ALSO BY MARGARET SHEFFIELD AND SHEILA BEWLEY

Where Do Babies Come From?

Before You Were Born

Life Blood

Life Blood

A NEW IMAGE FOR MENSTRUATION

Margaret Sheffield

Illustrated By
Sheila Bewley

ALFRED A. KNOPF

NEW YORK 1989

THIS IS A BORZOI BOOK
PUBLISHED BY ALFRED A. KNOPF, INC.

Copyright © 1988 by Margaret Sheffield and Sheila Bewley

All rights reserved under International and Pan-American Copyright
Conventions. Published in the United States by Alfred A. Knopf, Inc.,
New York. Distributed by Random House, Inc.,
New York. Originally published in Great Britain by Jonathan Cape
Ltd, London, in 1988.

Library of Congress Cataloging-in-Publication Data

Sheffield, Margaret.
Life blood.

1. Menstruation—Popular works.   I. Bewley,
Sheila.   II. Title.
QP263.S54   1989   612'.662   87-46237
ISBN 0-394-57065-0

Manufactured in the United States of America
First American Edition

Life Blood

Menstruation is a common fact of life.
From the very beginning female bodies are
equipped with their own internal systems
for the survival of the human race.

Menstruation happens to all women.
It happened to our mothers and grandmothers
and to all our female ancestors throughout history,
and it starts automatically as a girl grows up.

Flesh is beautiful, but opaque.
It covers us like our clothes,
keeping the rest of the body invisible
so that we can hardly imagine it.

Yet, inside the wall of skin,
the body is like the engine of a racing car,
strongly made and finely tuned.
Amazing feats of biology happen there every day.

There are millions of cells
in the human body.
Each one has a life of its own.

Together they make up all the
main parts of every human being
—man, woman, and child—
and they interact
with brilliant precision
to keep life going day after day.

But deep within the
complicated architecture
of the body is one system
that is special to women.

It is a hormone system
that starts up during puberty
and has major effects on the body.
On the outside, hormones make
the body change shape.

Inside, hormones create
a new routine involving
the ovaries and the uterus,
the two main parts
of the female body
which have to do
with reproduction.

Nature is amazingly prolific.
Girls are born with
enough tiny egg cells in
their ovaries to populate
a small town with people
if it were possible for every one
to grow into a baby
and be born.

At puberty the egg cells
begin to drift down
one by one
to the uterus.

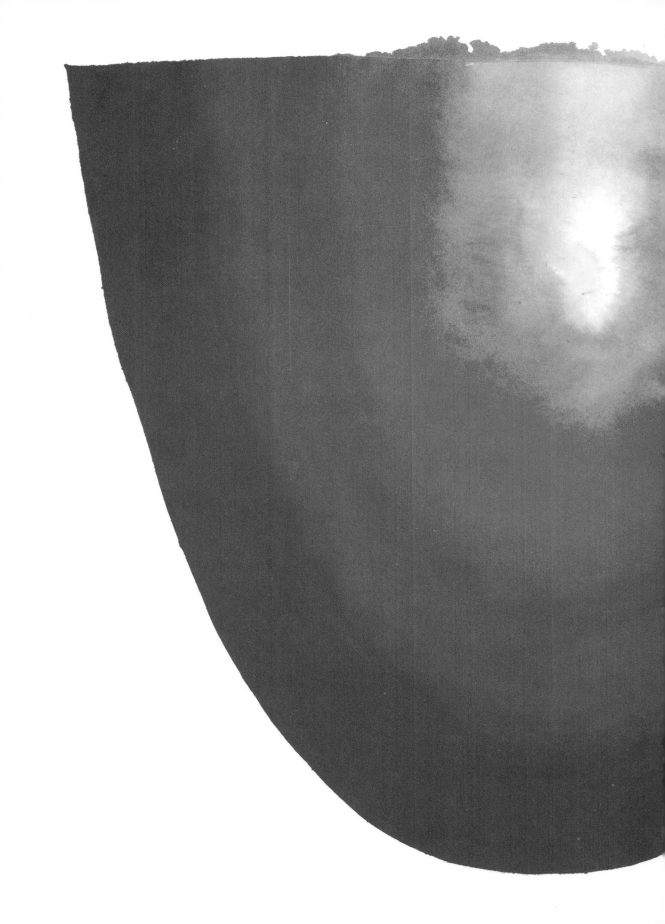

It takes
about four weeks
for an egg cell
to travel from an
ovary to the uterus.
Every four weeks
another one sets out.
Every four weeks
the uterus prepares for the
egg cell by developing
a blood-red lining,
like a room being painted
for a new occupant.

But most egg cells
don't stay in the uterus.
They dissolve into nothing and
disappear, and the lining of the uterus
breaks up and begins to pass away.
This is the cause of menstruation.

If menstruation was like
some other systems
in the body, there would
be no sign that it
was happening.
But it is different because
the blood that made up
the uterus' lining
comes out of the body
through the vagina.

Women call this
"having a period"—
and they get very expert
at dealing with them.

Periods last for a
few days every month.

Menstrual blood is not exactly like
the blood in the veins and the arteries.

During each period it has to be absorbed
by tampons or sanitary napkins.

Sometimes menstrual blood is pink, sometimes it's
scarlet, sometimes it's purple-black or reddish-brown.

It's the special blood in which
all our lives started.

To understand menstruation
is to understand the origins
of life in the uterus.

During pregancy women
don't have periods.
Then, instead of passing away
as menstrual blood,
the lining of the uterus
develops into the placenta.

Before we were born,
each of us needed this
placenta to keep alive.
It nourished us with
food and oxygen.
It was joined to us by
the umbilical cord,
and we were only separated
from it after birth
when the cord was cut.

Menstruation is a vital part of every woman's life experience,
whether she is married or unmarried,
and whether she is going to have babies or not.
After its beginning as a girl is growing up,
it goes on a regular schedule for the next
thirty to forty years before it stops.

It's one of the essential processes
of human biology.

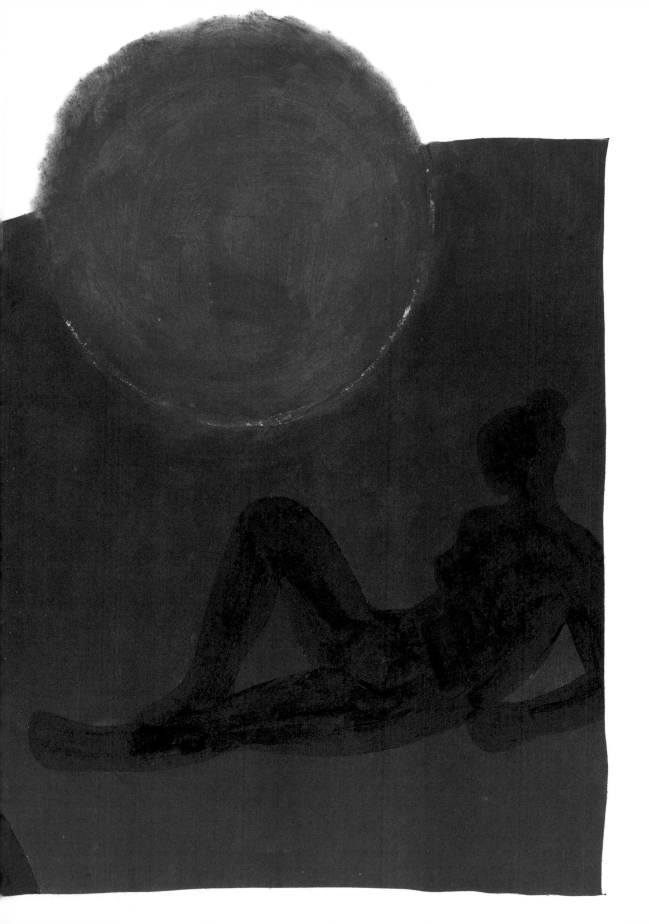

What do these words mean?

Biology   The knowledge and science of living things. The "biology" of a living thing is how it is made and how it works.

Cell   A cell is the basic unit of living matter. Human bodies are made of cells, which are continually reproducing themselves.

Egg cell   A special kind of cell that contains half the genetic material required to start a new baby. Egg cells are tiny specks of matter, which can really be seen only with a microscope.

Hormones   Natural substances, made by various glands in the body, which have specific effects on certain body processes. One hormone, estrogen, causes the ovaries to release their egg cells. Another, progesterone, causes the uterus to develop its lining. Hormones are sometimes called nature's "messengers" because they "tell" other parts of the body when to do things.

Menstruation   The natural monthly flow of blood from the uterus passing out of the body through the vagina.

Ovaries   There are two ovaries, one on each side of the uterus, to which they are connected by tubes. Ovaries are the female reproductive organs, equivalent to the testicles of men. Ovaries contain egg cells and manufacture the hormone estrogen.

Period   To "have a period" means to menstruate. It is the usual term to use. Menstruation happens "periodically"—every four weeks.

Placenta   The placenta is the unborn baby's life support system, providing it with oxygen and food from the mother's bloodstream. It is a dark, blood-colored mass (rather like a plate of liver), which develops from the lining of the uterus when a woman is pregnant, and which stays in the uterus until the baby is born.

Puberty   The period of sexual development at the beginning of adolescence which culminates, in girls, in the onset of menstruation.

Reproduction   All plants and animals have ways of making sure that their species does not end with their own deaths. They reproduce themselves. Reproduction in human beings begins with an act of sexual intercourse between a man and a woman in which a sperm cell fertilizes an egg cell while it is still in the woman's body.

Umbilical cord   The cord that connects the unborn child to the placenta and thus to the body of the mother. It is tied and cut at birth.

Uterus   Also called the womb. The part of the body in which a baby grows before it is born, and where the blood of menstruation comes from.

Vagina   The way out of the body from the uterus.

A Note on the Type

This book was set in Novarese, created by the European designer
Aldo Novarese, well known for such typefaces as Eurostile, Egizio,
Torino and Nova Augustea.
Novarese's distinctive, classic style is derived from its graceful
curves and finely chiseled serifs. The contrast between its thick and
thin strokes is noticeable but not extreme, giving the text a sparkle
without sacrificing readability.

Composed by Maxwell Photographics, New York, New York. Printed
by National Litho, Baltimore, Maryland. Bound by Bookbinders, Inc.,
Jersey City, New Jersey.

Typography and binding design by Mia Vander Els